ANDARD

TO SCHOOL

A PRACTICAL GUIDE TO
RACIAL EQUALITY IN
EARLY CHILDHOOD
EDUCATION AND CARE

UNITING BRITAIN

COMMISSION FOR
RACIAL EQUALITY

FOR A JUST SOCIETY

The Commission for Racial Equality

is working for a just society

which gives everyone an equal chance

to learn, work and live

free from discrimination and prejudice

and from the fear

of racial harassment

and violence

© Commission for Racial Equality
Elliot House
10/12 Allington Street
London SW1E 5EH

Revised edition 1996

ISBN 1 85442 021 6
Price: £5.00

Printed by Belmont Press

CONTENTS

Article 2 of the United Nations Convention on the Rights of the Child

1. *States Parties shall respect and ensure the rights set forth in the present Convention to each child within their jurisdiction without discrimination of any kind, irrespective of the child's or his or her parent's or legal guardian's race, colour, sex, language, religion, political or other opinion, national, ethnic or social origin, property, disability, birth or other status.*

2. *States Parties shall take all appropriate measures to ensure that the child is protected against all forms of discrimination or punishment on the basis of the status, activities, expressed opinions, or beliefs of the child's parents, legal guardians, or family members.*

FOREWORD

I f we are to break the cycle of racial inequality and prejudice, we need to strive to eliminate discrimination at all ages and stages of a child's development. This guide is a contribution to that task. It shows how the Race Relations Act 1976 and the Children Act 1989 apply to young children and to those who have responsibility for their care and education.

The Children Act 1989 is a comprehensive piece of legislation on the care of children, which addresses the questions of a 'child's religious persuasion, racial origin and cultural and linguistic background'. In terms of ensuring equality in childcare and educational provision and practice generally, it adds to the specific requirements of the Race Relations Act 1976. Local authorities need to consider racial equality issues in the registration, inspection and review of day care.

Over recent years, there has been increasing recognition that in a multicultural, multifaith and multilingual society, the needs of all children should be addressed positively. However, there is less certainty about how to go about doing so.

This guide is intended to help all those who work with young children and care for them to ensure that children from all ethnic groups start their lives on an equal footing. Today's children will be tomorrow's adults, and it is our responsibility to make sure they grow up free of racial prejudice, so that they can play their part as responsible citizens in a just, tolerant and diverse society.

Herman Ouseley
Chairman, Commission for Racial Equality

INTRODUCTION

The importance of a child's early years as a basis for all-round development is now widely recognised. Less well understood, however, are the implications for race relations.

In October 1991, the 1989 Children Act came into effect. While the full implications of this law will not become clear for some time, the Act, along with its accompanying Guidance on education and day care, provides a positive framework for good practice on racial equality issues for the early years, and reinforces the CRE's statutory duty to 'promote equality of opportunity, and good relations, between persons of different racial groups'.

Later that year, in December 1991, the United Kingdom ratified the UN Convention on the Rights of the Child, which includes key articles (see Appendix A) on the importance of racial equality issues.

In 1994, the Government responded to the long-standing campaign by organisations and individuals to increase nursery provision, and made a commitment to provide nursery education for all four-year-olds whose parents wanted it. However, while there have been welcome changes recently with respect to racial equality, any general expansion of provision will have to be accompanied by substantial changes in practice if all young children, whatever their ethnic origins, are to benefit equally.

In the context of these developments, this guide spells out the relevance of both the Race Relations Act 1976 and the Children Act 1989 to early years services. The guide examines existing provision and the extent to which it meets the needs of ethnic minority communities. It then goes on to highlight key areas where a commitment to racial equality policies and practices would benefit all the children involved. Finally, it discusses the issues of access to services, training and employment. The guide concludes by suggesting ways in which policies might be developed to ensure that all aspects of early childhood services are founded on the principles of equality of opportunity and freedom from racial prejudice and discrimination.

The practice, organisation and language of early childhood services vary throughout Britain. Scottish legislation is different in important respects. We have tried as far as possible, to take account of these variations in the text. The Equal Opportunities Commission has produced a parallel guide on how to ensure sex equality, *An Equal Start: Guidelines on equal treatment for the under eights,* and the two booklets may be used together to develop programmes and policies to tackle racial and sex discrimination and inequality.

This guide is aimed at all those who educate and care for young children, whether as parents or professionals, both in multiracial, inner-city areas and in those parts of Britain where the ethnic minority population is small. It is addressed to those who make, develop and monitor policy about young children; those who administer, manage, inspect and register early childhood services; and advisers, educators, trainers and employees in professional, statutory, private and voluntary organisations.

EARLY CHILDHOOD SERVICES AND THE 1976 RACE RELATIONS ACT

The Race Relations Act (RRA) affects early childhood services in many ways through its provisions on education, employment, local authorities, training, services, advertising and special needs. This chapter summarises the scope of the RRA in this field.

Employment and training matters are addressed in detail in the CRE *Code of Practice ... in Employment* (CRE, 1984), which has been approved by Parliament. The Code explains the provisions of the Race Relations Act and makes recommendations on the policies needed to eliminate racial discrimination in employment and to promote equality of opportunity.

The CRE has also issued a *Code of Practice for the Elimination of Racial Discrimination in Education* (CRE, 1989 and CRE, 1991a), which makes recommendations on the policies needed to avoid racial discrimination and ensure equality of opportunity in education and childcare services.

The RRA gives people who believe they have been discriminated against on racial grounds in the area of employment the right to bring their complaint before an industrial tribunal. Complaints of discrimination in other areas are heard in county courts in England and Wales and in sheriff courts in Scotland. The CRE has the sole power to bring proceedings in cases of discriminatory advertisements or instructions or pressure to discriminate. The CRE also has the power to conduct formal investigations. For details about law enforcement under the Race Relations Act see Appendix B.

The Race Relations Act defines racial discrimination as less favourable treatment on racial grounds, and identifies several ways in which such treatment might occur.

Direct discrimination (Section 1 (1)(a))

This means treating a person less favourably on racial grounds than another person is, or would be, treated in the same or similar circumstances. It should be noted that the motive or intention behind such treatment is irrelevant.

Examples

- It would be unlawful for a playgroup, nursery or childminder to refuse to admit a child simply because she or he is black or white.

- It would be unlawful for a childminder, playgroup or nursery to discriminate against a particular racial group[1] in the access provided to certain activities or facilities. For instance, the stereotyped assumption that Afro-Caribbean boys lack concentration might lead a nursery, playgroup or childminder to let them play continuously on mobile toys such as bicycles while encouraging other children to develop a wider variety of cognitive learning skills.

- It would be unlawful to give a child on the waiting list of a nursery or playgroup preference solely because of his or her racial group, even if the nursery's aim was to reflect the ethnic composition of the community or to have a multiracial group.

---

1 A racial group is a group defined by reference to race, colour, nationality,citizenship or ethnic or national origins. The House of Lords ruled in *Mandla v Dowell Lee* (1983) that this definition included groups with a 'long shared history' and a 'cultural tradition' of their own, among other factors; for example Sikhs. In 1988 the Court of Appeal ruled that Romany Gypsies constitute a racial group.

- It would be unlawful for a nursery or playgroup to set racial quotas for children, or reserve places on a racial basis.

Segregation (Section 1(2))

Segregating a person from others on racial grounds constitutes less favourable treatment.

Example

- Grouping children for play activities or at mealtime according to their racial group, and for no other reason, would be unlawful.

Indirect discrimination (Section 1(1)(b))

This means applying a requirement or condition which, although applied equally to all racial groups, is such that a considerably smaller proportion of a particular racial group can comply with it, is to that group's detriment, and cannot be shown to be justifiable on non-racial grounds

Customs, practices and procedures which may have been in place for a long time may have an indirectly discriminatory effect on particular racial groups, even though that was never the intention.

Examples

- In the case of *Mandla v Dowell Lee* in 1983, a school made it compulsory to wear a cap as part of a school uniform. The rule had the effect of excluding Sikh boys, who are required by their faith to wear a turban. The House of Lords decided that the rule was not justifiable, and constituted unlawful indirect discrimination.

- It may be indirectly discriminatory to make it a requirement for someone to have a specific qualification or experience in

11

order to work in a nursery or playgroup or apply for a training course, unless it can be shown that the requirement is essential for the job or training, or that it is laid down by statute, for example, qualified teacher status. In the case of *Arshad v Newcastle upon Tyne City Council (1989)*, a teaching qualification was made a prerequisite for the post of a language coordinator, and this was ruled to be indirectly discriminatory. It is nearly always possible to avoid this situation by listing a particular qualification or experience and then adding, 'or other relevant or appropriate qualifications or experience', so that no one is prevented from applying on racial grounds.

● Giving preference to applicants to a nursery from a particular catchment area, if this unjustifiably excludes an area where people from a particular racial group live, could be indirectly discriminatory.

● Requiring children to pass a language screening test in order to be accepted for admission to a mainstream school may disproportionately affect particular racial groups. The CRE's formal investigation into second language provision in Calderdale (CRE, 1986) found that this amounted to unlawful indirect racial discrimination. Such provision was to the pupils' detriment and could not be justified on non-racial (that is, educational) grounds.

Victimisation (Section 2)

A person is victimised if he or she is treated less favourably than others in the same circumstances because it is suspected or known that he or she has brought proceedings under the Race Relations Act, or given evidence or information concerning such proceedings, or alleged that discrimination has occurred.

Example

- Refusing a child a nursery place because his or her parents have previously complained about racial discrimination at the nursery would be unlawful.

The following sections of the Race Relations Act are also relevant to early childhood services, and define other circumstances in which unlawful discrimination might occur.

Discriminatory practices (Section 28)

It is unlawful to operate a practice which calls for the imposition of a condition or requirement that is, or would be, indirectly discriminatory if there were any occasion for applying it.

Example

- It would be unlawful to have an indirectly discriminatory rule about the type of clothes children should wear at the nursery, even if there are no applicants at present from the racial group that might be affected.

Instructions or pressure to discriminate (Sections 30 and 31)

It is unlawful to instruct or put pressure on others to discriminate unlawfully on racial grounds.

Examples

- A board of governors or management committee would be breaking the law if it instructed the person in charge of a nursery or playgroup not to accept any Bangladeshi children.

- It would be unlawful to instruct the person responsible for work experience placements for students not to send someone from a particular racial group to a specific placement.

The reasons for such an instruction, for example, they thought the placement would be 'unsuitable' for students from that racial group, are irrelevant.

- It would be unlawful for a group of parents to petition a nursery not to admit children from a particular racial group. Similarly, it would be unlawful for a childminder to ask the local social services department not to send them a child from a particular racial group.

- Pressure to discriminate could also include the staff of a nursery asking their coordinator not to appoint a manager from a particular racial group. Again, the reasons for this action are irrelevant.

Aiding unlawful acts (Section 33)

A person who knowingly assists someone to discriminate unlawfully on racial grounds will be equally liable under the RRA, unless they can show that they had been told by the other party that the action was lawful, and it was reasonable for them to rely on that statement.

Example

- A local authority would be in breach of the RRA if it registered a childminder as a fit person to look after children under the age of eight (under the Children Act 1989) and was aware that the childminder would refuse to look after children from a particular racial group, and/or that any other person in the childminder's household refused to have such children in the home.

Advertisements (Section 29)

It is generally unlawful to publish an advertisement which might reasonably be understood to indicate an intention to discriminate, whether or not the discrimination would be unlawful, unless the act of discrimination is covered by certain specific exemptions from the Act (see p 18). 'Advertisement' is defined very widely to include all forms of advertisement or notice, whether to the public or not (see Section 78 of the RRA). All press, TV and radio advertising is covered. The RRA also covers the display of notices, signs, labels, cards or goods, the distribution of circulars, pictures and so on (CRE, 1994a).

Examples

● It would be unlawful to publish a list of childminders which indicated that they were only prepared to mind children from a particular racial group.

● It would be unlawful to publish guidelines for admission to a nursery or playgroup which included racially discriminatory criteria.

Charities (Section 34)

A charity acting within the terms of its charitable instrument is exempt from the RRA, provided that the charitable instrument does not discriminate on grounds of colour.

Example

● If a nursery is established under a charitable instrument whose aims are to provide education for French children, this is not unlawful. If, however, the instrument refers to white French children, the reference to 'white' must be disregarded.

It should be remembered, however, that the general exemption will not apply if the charity goes beyond its charitable instrument, nor does it apply in relation to its wider responsibilities, for example, as an employer.

Education (Sections 17, 18 and 19)

Section 17 makes it unlawful for an educational establishment, including nursery schools and classes and institutions of further and higher education, to discriminate in admission (including any conditions of admission), exclusion, providing access to any benefits, facilities or services, or subjecting a child or student to any other detriment.

Section 18 makes it unlawful for a local education authority to discriminate on racial grounds in carrying out any of its functions under the Education Acts between 1944 and 1993 (in Scotland, the Education (Scotland) Acts between 1939 and 1980) that are not covered by Section 17.

Section 19 gives education authorities a general duty not to discriminate on racial grounds in the provision of educational facilities and ancillary benefits or services.

Employment (Sections 4, 12, 32)

Section 4 of the RRA makes it unlawful for an employer to discriminate on racial grounds in recruitment, selection, conditions of employment, promotion, dismissal, training, transfer or providing access to any other benefits, facilities or services. This covers not only staff in childcare or educational establishments but also trainers, support staff, advisory and administrative employees and those from external support agencies, such as speech therapists.

Section 12 makes it unlawful for a body conferring qualifications for a profession or trade to discriminate in the granting of that qualification or in the terms on which it is granted. This covers bodies such as the Council for Awards in Children's Care and Education (incorporating the Council for Early Years Awards (CEYA) and the National Nursery Examination Board (NNEB)), the Central Council for Education and Training in Social Work (CCETSW), the Business and Technical Education Council (BTEC), the City and Guilds of London Institute and the Scottish

Vocational Education Council (SCOTVEC).

Section 32 makes an employer liable for any act of discrimination by an employee, even if it was performed without the employer's knowledge or consent, unless it can be shown that all reasonable steps were taken to prevent the employee from discriminating.

Example

- If staff employed by a local authority to run a community centre refuse to hire a room to an Asian parents' group on racial grounds, the local authority could be liable for this apparent act of discrimination.

Vocational Training (Section 13)

Section 13 makes it unlawful for a vocational training body to discriminate on racial grounds against a person who is seeking or undergoing training (including, in some circumstances, work experience) in the following ways: in the terms on which they are afforded access; by refusing or deliberately omitting to afford them access; by terminating the training; or by subjecting them to any other detriment in the course of the training.

Example

- It would be unlawful for a nursery employee to racially abuse a nursery nurse student on a training placement in the nursery.

Services (Section 20)

Section 20 makes it unlawful for anyone providing goods, facilities or services to the public, or a section of the public, to discriminate by deliberately omitting or refusing to provide the same goods, facilities or services to a person on racial grounds, or by providing them in a less favourable manner or on worse terms. This covers the goods, facilities and services provided to young children and their families in day nurseries, family centres, combined nursery centres, drop-in centres, community or workplace nurseries, playgroups, crêches, parent and toddler clubs, playbuses, after-school care, childminders, childminder support groups and voluntary, private, and statutory organisations responsible for any childcare facilities.

Section 20 does not apply, however, where a person takes children into their home and treats them as if they were members of the family, whether for payment or not (Section 23(2)). This would clearly cover foster carers. However, both the CRE and the National Childminding Association (NCMA) take the view that the service provided by childminders cannot be described as treating children as if they were members of the family in the same way as foster carers. In its *Second Review of the Race Relations Act*, the CRE recommended that Section 23(2) be amended in so far as it is necessary to clarify its non-application to registered childminders. At the time of writing, this recommendation had been accepted by the government but legislation to implement it had not been published. (See page 48 for further discussion of the application of the RRA and the Children Act to childminding).

Associations (Section 26)

It is not unlawful to form an 'association' with the main object of enabling the benefits of membership to be enjoyed by people of a particular racial group, so long as this is not defined by reference to colour. Such an association could run a nursery or playgroup solely for the use of its members.

Example

● An Irish community centre or a synagogue can lawfully run a playgroup only for its members' children.

Exemptions from the Act (Sections 4(3), 5, 35, 37, 38)

There are a number of ways in which the RRA permits lawful discrimination on racial grounds. Although strictly limited, the exemptions are intended to mitigate the consequences of past discrimination. The exemptions also seek to take account of certain specific circumstances.

Employment

- It is lawful for an employer or any person or training body to encourage applications from a particular racial group, or make training facilities available only to people from a particular racial group, where it can be shown that members of that racial group have been underrepresented in the work in question for the previous 12 months (Sections 37 and 38). Where these sections have been used, however, it would be unlawful for an employer actually to appoint a person solely on racial grounds. The Race Relations Employment Advisory Service has produced a useful guide to this area of legislation and practice, *Positive Action, Promoting racial equality in employment.*[2]

- It is lawful to recruit someone from a particular racial group where being from that group is a 'genuine occupational qualification'. For example, nursery care or education for a group of children which includes a large number from a particular racial group may well be most effectively provided with the assistance of someone from that group who understands its language, culture, religion, home life, and family relationships. Caring for these children and their families without regard to such factors may not be conducive to their welfare. However, this section does not apply in the following circumstances: an employer already has employees from the racial

---

2 Available free from Cambertown Ltd, Unit 8, Goldthorpe Industrial Estate, Goldthorpe, Rotherham, South Yorkshire S63 9BL

group in question who are capable of carrying out the required duties; it would be reasonable to employ them on those duties; and there are sufficient numbers available not unduly to inconvenience the employer. (Section 5)

- It is lawful, when employing someone to work in a private household, for example as nannies, au pairs or mother's helps, to select applicants on the grounds of their racial group. (Section 4(3))

Employment, education, facilities and services

- It may be lawful to take action to meet the special needs of a particular racial group in regard to their education, training or welfare, or any ancillary benefits, according to the particular circumstances. For example, it may be lawful to provide information or facilities to meet those special needs, such as bilingual early years workers; or an early years project for refugees (and possibly their families) to address their recent experiences and the new context of their lives. (Section 35)

Local authorities

Section 71 of the Act places a duty on local authorities to carry out their various functions 'with due regard to the need (a) to eliminate unlawful racial discrimination; and (b) to promote equality of opportunity, and good race relations, between persons of different racial groups'.

For example, several social services departments have set up language units to translate relevant information into the various languages spoken in the area, and provide interpreting services. Some have taken specific action to recruit childminders from racial groups underrepresented in their list of registered childminders compared with the ethnic composition of the local population.

In those local authorities where nursery provision is not universally available, this duty should ensure that when any expansion or cuts in services are being planned, special attention is paid to the siting of provision, in order to ensure equal access for children from all racial groups.

Ethnic monitoring

It is not possible to be sure that employers or providers of a service, however good their policies, are not discriminating on racial grounds unless data on people's ethnic origins is collected and analysed at key stages of the decision-making processes. Ethnic data should be collected on:

- applications, selection and admission for all early childhood services

- applications, shortlisting and employment offers for all posts in the organisation and delivery of early childhood services.

The data needs to be analysed, and any racial or ethnic disparities examined. While such disparities may be caused by a variety of factors, any practices or procedures that are unlawfully discriminatory must be changed.

The CRE has published booklets (CRE, 1991c and 1992b) on ethnic monitoring in employment and in education which should be helpful in preparing for the Three-Yearly Review required by the Children Act. This review provides an opportunity to collect ethnic data on employment and service delivery, perhaps focusing on the recruitment and selection of those who work with children, and on applications and admissions to early childhood provision as initial priorities. (See page 27 for details.)

EARLY CHILDHOOD SERVICES AND THE CHILDREN ACT 1989

The Children Act 1989 and its accompanying Guidance (HMSO, 1991) makes specific reference to a child's 'religious persuasion, racial origin and cultural and linguistic background'. It is clear from the spirit of the Act that 'day care' means both 'education' and 'care' in all forms of provision for children under the age of eight.

In England and Wales, the Children Act places a duty on local authorities to 'safeguard and promote the welfare of children ... in need'. They have a duty to provide day care for such children 'as appropriate', whether over or under the age of five, and 'may' also make provision for those not in need. In relation to day care, the Act requires local authorities to work in partnership in supporting families; to take account of the views of children and parents; to consult individual departments (social services, education and health) and voluntary organisations; and to provide comprehensive information on the statutory and voluntary services for children under eight.

In England, Wales and Scotland, the Act gives local authorities powers to set basic standards of care for those children up to the age of eight who are looked after for more than two hours a day; to make changes to the system of registering and deregistering day care providers; and to require an inspection of services at least once a year. Education departments should help and support social services departments in establishing, developing and inspecting such services. The Act requires local authority education and social services departments to produce a Three-Yearly Review of all day care provision for children under eight in the area, in consultation with health authorities and others (Section 19). The results of each review must be published.

Section 22(5)(c) of the Children Act requires local authorities, in making any decision with respect to a child in their care, to give 'due consideration to the child's religious persuasion, racial origin and cultural and linguistic background'.

Section 74(6) requires local authorities to 'have regard to the child's religious persuasion, racial origin and cultural and linguistic background' in considering whether the day care provided is 'seriously inadequate', in terms of the needs of a child, and whether to cancel registration.

The duties on local authorities are consistent with the duties on a court to make a child's welfare its paramount consideration when determining any question concerning the child's upbringing. One of the relevant considerations in determining a child's best interest is 'the child's... background and any characteristics of his which the court considers relevant...' (Section 1(3)(d)). There is no specific reference to race or religion, but these would be included under Section 1(3)(d). The welfare checklist is applied in most private and public law proceedings.

In making arrangements for the provision of day care (and encouraging people to be foster parents), Schedule 2, paragraph 11 requires local authorities, to 'have regard to the different racial groups to which children within their area who are in need belong'.

What the Guidance says

Local authorities 'should provide a range of services which should reflect (in scale as well as type) the needs of children and families from ethnic minority groups' (para 2.12). The text throughout refers to the need to take account of cultural and linguistic needs (for example, by using interpreters and translators), to ensure that ethnic minority groups are consulted about policy and practice, and that the resources and food provided are appropriate to the children's cultural and religious backgrounds.

The chapter on standards in education and day care services states that the 'values deriving from different backgrounds –

racial, cultural, religious and linguistic – should be recognised and respected' (para 6.2). This is further elaborated in a section called 'Equal opportunities and racial groups':

> (each child should be) valued as an individual without racial stereotyping. Children from a very young age learn about different races and cultures including religion and languages and will be capable of assigning different values to them.... It is important that people working with young children are aware of this, so that their practice enables the children to develop positive attitudes to differences of race, culture and language' (para 6.10).

It goes on to say that local authorities should have

> approved equal opportunity policies including arrangements for monitoring and reviewing progress towards implementation ... (and) ensure that they have available data on the ethnic origins of the local population which is essential for assessment of the extent to which the day care and educational services.... are operating in a non-discriminatory way (para 6.11).

They should also ensure that all racial groups are able to take part in consultation about the review process.

In describing the quality of care, the Guidance discusses children's 'right to an environment which facilitates their development', including being 'part of a community which values the religious, racial, cultural and linguistic identity of the child' in terms of 'fostering the child's sense of identity'. Other rights include 'freedom from discrimination such as racism' (para 6.28).

Children in need

The definition of 'need' includes needs associated with the child's 'race, religion, culture and language' (para 2.4). Thus a local authority definition of children in need could include refugee children; homeless children; children who receive free school meals; children in poor housing (who, in many areas, are disproportionately from ethnic minority groups); children subjected to racial harassment; and children learning English as a second language. (This last group is specifically excluded from the definition of 'special educational needs' in the 1981 Education Act as learning difficulties which call for special educational provision). In making arrangements for day care, local authorities will need to take account of current needs, analysed by ethnic group, as well as anticipate future needs. Existing lists of service providers should be examined, and steps taken to ensure that they and, where possible, the children in their provision, reflect the ethnic composition of the local population (see Macdonald, 1991).

Cancellation of registration

'Failure to recognise and respond sensitively to a child's religious, racial, cultural and linguistic needs' is cited as one of the grounds on which local authorities may cancel the registration of a day care provider or childminder. Local authorities are asked to consider whether such failure constitutes 'less favourable treatment on racial grounds', whether the child is 'being ridiculed', or whether the child's 'dietary needs' are being met (para 7.52 (b)).

Registration of day care

The Children Act refers specifically to the need to take account of 'a child's religious persuasion, racial origin and cultural and linguistic background' in considering whether care is sufficiently inadequate to cancel registration. 'Seriously inadequate' care may be care that was originally defined as 'inadequate', but has since become 'seriously inadequate' because nothing was done about this.

The Guidance suggests that local authorities consider the following points when determining whether a person is fit (that is 'suitable') to 'look after children aged under eight', and/or whether other people living or working on the premises are 'fit to be in the proximity of children aged under eight'.

● 'knowledge of and attitude to multicultural issues and people of different racial origins'; and

- 'commitment and knowledge to treat all children as individuals and with equal concern' (para 7.32).

Together with the specific registration guidelines or criteria used by the local authority, these two points provide a basis on which to make decisions about who should be refused registration, and what training and support needs have been identified:

- First, those in breach of the Race Relations Act should be refused registration – for example, those who refuse admission on racial grounds or instruct others to do so; those who treat children from particular racial groups less favourably, on racial grounds, in a playgroup, childminding, or nursery setting; or those who make discriminatory admission arrangements (see also chapters 1 and 5).

- Second, local authorities need to consider whether to register a person who refuses to promote equality of opportunity in terms of their own registration criteria and the issues raised in the Guidance. While these issues may simply be new to some people, who will need training and support to further their development in practical ways, others may be unwilling or unable to address them.

It is important, whenever possible, to involve policy makers, administrators, trainers, practitioners (from education, leisure and social services departments), lawyers and elected members in the process of developing local authority registration criteria. Only by discussing and debating the issues involved will the rationale behind them be fully understood.

One way to evaluate the quality of care with regard to children's religious persuasion, racial origin and cultural and linguistic background is to define practice in terms of specific elements, for example, resources, admissions, activities, health and 'ethos', and then to assess a person's competence in each area on a range from good to poor. Evaluating the quality of care in this way requires considerable skill and is time-consuming, but setting specific criteria by which to judge it avoids the possibility of basing decisions on hunches and stereotypes (Early Childhood Unit, National Children's Bureau, 1995). In addition, self-evaluation is important, particularly as it helps those involved to learn what is involved in good practice to eliminate racial discrimination, acknowledge problems and accept support where necessary. Several organisations have developed guidelines for good practice in which racial equality issues are integral – see the list of useful organisations at the end of this booklet.

The Three-Yearly Review

The Children Act says that the Three-Yearly Review of all day care provision (including the number of children in LEA nursery schools and classes) should be undertaken jointly by the LEA and the social services department. This must be an 'open process' involving all relevant interests and groups (health authorities, voluntary organisations, employer interests, parents and other interested bodies and individuals), including ethnic minority groups, to give their views on existing patterns of services, the need for change, and how this might be instituted. Specifically, 'the concept of "review" involves measurement or assessment' and is 'not possible without agreed aims and objectives for the services' (para 9.10). The consultative process may include interpreting and translation services, but the arrangements should enable people from all ethnic groups to contribute fully.

Collection and analysis of ethnic data on the children using the provision, their carers and teachers, and the administrators is essential to identify any divorce between policy and practice. An analysis is also required of the curriculum provided, including 'multicultural and equal opportunities aspects'. The public report, which will provide the basis for evaluating whether the needs of ethnic minority families and their children are being met, should include an account of local equal opportunities policies. Where appropriate, it should be published in languages other than English.

The review provides a clear basis, for the first time, for an overall examination of early years services. It should provide evidence for questions about admissions policies, where and how vacancies are advertised, costs and opening hours, etc, in order to identify whether racial discrimination (direct or indirect) is a factor.

Once the concept of collecting and analysing ethnic data is understood and accepted, a framework can be developed for the information required, the data collected, and the results analysed. At the time of writing, most local authorities were only in the early stages of this process. In practice, the task is not very different from what they already do by way of collecting and monitoring information, but the Guidance requires the collection of this data in order to ensure that 'the educational and day care services are operating in a non-discriminatory way'. Monitoring existing policies and procedures is the only way of demonstrating that they are actually doing what they are intended to do. (See p 20 for information about ethnic monitoring and chapters 5, 6 & 7 for further discussion of the issues).

Specific issues arising from the Children Act

Registration and assessment of people who do not speak or read English.

Where possible this should be done by someone familiar with the carer's or educator's language, and with early childhood services generally, perhaps by 'sharing' staff with nearby authorities. In considering issues such as safety, care must be taken to define what is required to protect children and to see that the principles are applied on a non-discriminatory basis. For example, in applying principles of access to emergency services, which may require competence in numeracy and the English language, those who speak English, but cannot read or write it, are almost as disadvantaged as those who can only speak, read or write in a language other than English. Both need support in order to incorporate safety concerns and facilitate registration.

Registration of people and groups with specific religious beliefs.

The Race Relations Act does not cover discrimination on grounds of religion (see p 10, footnote 1). However, religion and race sometimes overlap. A religious organisation can run a nursery or playgroup solely for its members (under Section 26 of the Race Relations Act), provided that there is no discrimination on grounds of colour. The same applies to an association which is a charity. In such a situation, it will be up to a local authority to decide whether to register it under the Children Act according to its own criteria. In turn, this will depend in part on how the nursery or playgroup addresses issues of religion, racial origin or cultural or linguistic background.

Where a religious association's nursery or playgroup is not run mainly for its members' children, it must not exclude children on racial grounds – either directly or indirectly – through its admission arrangements, or treat children less favourably on racial grounds. The same applies where a nursery or playgroup is set up independent of any association, and the management and staff wish to maintain their religious practice in the nursery.

Example

A nursery is run on Christian lines, but it does not come within Section 26 of the RRA. Only Christian children are admitted, and Jewish, Hindu, and Muslim children are excluded. The legal position is as follows:

- *Jewish children.* Since Jews are a racial group under the Race Relations Act, this would be direct discrimination under Section 20.

- *Muslim and Hindu children.* This could constitute indirect discrimination under Section 20 if the children also belonged to a racial group (such as Pakistani or Bangladeshi) which was far less likely to be able to comply with the requirement of being Christian in order to gain admission. If the nursery can justify its requirement that the children should be Christian,

29

there is no breach of the Act. It is likely that statistical evidence of the disproportionately disadvantageous effect of the requirement would be needed. The existence of other available nurseries and playgroups in the area would also be taken into account.

In a nursery or playgroup where a particular faith is being practised, there is no provision under the Children Act for children to opt out of religious instruction or practice as children in maintained schools can under education legislation. All children are likely to be expected to take part in such instruction or practice, whatever their own faith. It is important, therefore, that those organising the nursery or playgroup spell out the religious practices of the nursery or playgroup to families thinking of sending a child there. If the group actively promotes one religion at the expense of others, a local authority may decide to refuse registration under the provisions of the Children Act. In particular, if children of faiths other than that of the organisers attend the nursery or playgroup, it would be open to the local authority to take the view that the care and education provided were 'seriously inadequate' in respect of meeting their religious needs.

In the case of a Muslim nursery or playgroup where non-Muslim children are required to take part in Muslim forms of worship, it may be considered that this constitutes indirect racial discrimination. Whether this was justified would depend on all the circumstances. Clearly, the principles outlined above apply whatever the faith of a nursery or playgroup organisation.

Many local authorities, in order to ensure compliance with the equal opportunity provisions of the Children Act, require childminders and day care providers to sign a declaration on equality of opportunity as part of the registration process. While it may be impossible to impose the signing of any declaration as a precondition of registration (signing or not signing cannot be read as an indication of whether or not a person is 'fit'), it could be a requirement imposed at the local authority's discretion after registration has been agreed. However, signing a declaration alone may not be enough. Discussion of its implications in practice, together with appropriate training, is desirable.

Some religious groups have been unwilling, for a variety of reasons, to sign a declaration stating that they are, in principle, willing to have regard to religious persuasions other than their own. There may be a case for requiring the signing of a declaration regarding racial origin and cultural and linguistic background as some form of commitment, and leaving the issue of religious persuasion to be decided according to the specific circumstances of each situation.

Education provision

The Children Act requires LEAs to take part in the review of all day care. Although, at present, the curriculum of LEA nursery schools and classes in England and Wales is devised locally, children over the age of five in maintained primary schools are subject to the national curriculum. Both should incorporate the 'race' issues raised in the Children Act and its Guidance. This is consistent with the requirements of the Education Reform Act 1988 regarding curriculum: it 'promotes the spiritual, moral, cultural, mental and physical development of pupils at the school and of society' (Section 1(2)). Furthermore, the former National Curriculum Council (whose functions are now the responsibility of the School Curriculum and Assessment Authority (SCAA)) advises in its guidance to schools that 'a commitment to providing equal opportunities for all pupils.... should permeate every aspect of the curriculum' (NCC, 1990a). Guidance (NCC, 1990b) also states that equal opportunities are concerned with ensuring that all pupils are educated in an awareness of their rights and responsibilities with respect to equality. 'Rights include civil, political, social and human rights, and how these may be violated by various forms of injustice, inequality and discrimination, including racism...' (For further information, see Runnymede Trust, 1993).

EARLY CHILDHOOD SERVICES AND ETHNIC MINORITY COMMUNITIES

Organisation of early childhood services

With rare exceptions (such as combined nursery centres), local education authorities (LEAs), health authorities, social services departments, voluntary and private organisations and sometimes individual employers are at present separately responsible for the various types of early childhood services, although the local authority has a responsibility to ensure minimum standards. The services provided vary considerably from one area to another. For example, most LEAs provide at least some nursery schools and classes, but a few provide none, which places obvious pressure on the voluntary and private sectors in those areas. Furthermore, the amount of private sector provision is rapidly increasing. Overall, social services departments provide relatively fewer places (in day nurseries) for young children, compared with all other forms of provision. For children under the age of two, childminding is the most common form of full-time day care available, and for children between the ages of three and five the most common form of provision is voluntary sector playgroups.

The need for a coordinated or integrated service has long been recognised both by national and local government, and some authorities are now organising all their provision under one department. Although the Children Act requires all local authority departments to consult each other, the general picture remains one of poor coordination between the different organisations involved, with each concentrating on its own particular type of provision, recruiting staff with different training and educational backgrounds and offering different conditions of service and career paths. Implementation of the Children Act should facilitate coordination, although recent education legislation concerning the local management of schools (LMS), and the transfer of many former LEA roles to individual governing bodies, may militate against this objective.

Existing provision and ethnic minority children

What are the consequences of all this for children from ethnic minority communities? How are their needs being met?

Any answers to this question must be seen in the context of the absence of a universal norm of what constitutes a 'family'. Family patterns are varied and changing among both white and ethnic minority groups, and it is important not to make unjustified assumptions about family life or child care needs.

The 1991 census showed that ethnic minority groups in Britain have a larger share of young people than the white population: 11.10% of the ethnic minority population as a whole, compared with 6.36% of the white population, were under five years old (NEMDA, 1993a). This suggests that ethnic minority households are more likely to need childcare services – but as research into various socio-economic factors shows, they are also less likely to be able to pay for them.

The risks of unemployment, low income, dependence on social security benefits, and poor health and housing are greater for people from ethnic minority groups, with Bangladeshis, Pakistanis and black people particularly badly affected, and women from these groups most likely to experience poverty (see Amin, 1992). This situation may be due partly to their geographic and economic segregation in traditionally low paid-industries and in semi-skilled and unskilled jobs, and partly to racial discrimination and disadvantage (Kumar, 1993) For example, research shows that:

- Ethnic minority men and women are more likely than white men and women to work unsocial hours, doing shift work (Jones, 1993).

- A greater proportion of black and Indian mothers of children under five (whether they are lone parents or not) are employed, compared with other groups (DE, 1988; LFS, 1989-91).

- Just over half of West Indian, African and white mothers of children under eight are employed, but white mothers are more likely to work part-time (OPCS, 1994).[3]

- The ethnic minority unemployment rate at 18.8% is more than twice the rate for white people, at 8.1%. Pakistanis and Bangladeshis currently have the highest rate (27.3%) followed closely by black people (24.2%) (TUC, 1995a).

- Average national hourly rates of pay for people from ethnic minorities were 10% less than for white people (TUC, 1995b).

- Black families are about four times as likely as white families to be one-parent families (NEMDA, 1993b). Half of all black mothers are lone mothers compared to 14% of white mothers (Bartholomew et al, 1992; OPCS, 1994).

- Local studies provide evidence that ethnic minority households (including refugees and asylum-seekers) are overrepresented among the homeless; for example they formed 53% of those registered homeless in 1992/3 in London, while comprising only 15% of all households (LRC, 1994). Much of the accommodation for homeless families is temporary and unsatisfactory, and the need for childcare is likely to be that much greater.

---

3 The OPCS categories are: White, Black-Caribbean, Black-African, Black-Other, Indian, Pakistani, Bangladeshi, Chinese, Other-Asian, Other-Other.

- 70% of West Indian or African children under the age of eight live in rented accommodation compared with 26% of white children. Nearly all West Indian or African children (98%) live in urban areas compared with 63% of white children (OPCS, 1994).

There is now a large body of evidence to show that educational achievement is positively influenced by access to good early childhood care and education (House of Commons, 1989, and NCE, 1993). It would be comforting to believe that there is no difference in the quality of educational foundation laid by different types of early childhood services, but differences do exist. For example, although a place in an LEA nursery school generally costs less than a place in a social services day nursery, there are worries that the quality of some social services provision and some private and voluntary sector childcare services may not match what an LEA can offer in such respects as staff training and access to equipment.

Differences in training relate to the traditional distinction between 'education' and 'care'. Nursery teachers are trained to encourage the sequential, cognitive development of three- to seven-year-olds, while nursery nurses focus more on the all-round development of the under-fives. This can often mean a difference of emphasis for the three to five year olds, depending on whether nursery teachers or nursery nurses are in charge. Many nursery teachers and nurses would reject the artificial divide between 'care' and 'education' and all aim to provide a quality service. But what is provided by social services, private and voluntary sectors largely depends on the training and experience of the workers involved.

Although both nursery nurses and teachers may be offered the opportunity to obtain relevant experience and in-service training for work in multiracial urban situations, some day nurseries, with their emphasis on care, may not provide the same opportunities for planned cognitive, social and emotional development as nursery schools or classes. Children from day nurseries may therefore be at a disadvantage when they transfer to primary school. For example, as well as opportunities for active learning and free play activities, children need skilled educators to support and extend their learning. Observation and assessment of each child's understanding, skills, attitudes and feelings are part of planning an appropriate curriculum for children which will provide a firm foundation for the national curriculum followed in primary schools.

The evidence suggests that children with the greatest need have least access to those early childhood services best equipped to provide educational support (Sylva et al, 1992). This has clear implications for equal opportunities. If ethnic minority children are disproportionately concentrated in some types of services there is legitimate concern that they will begin their statutory schooling at some disadvantage.

Comprehensive data on the types of service used by children from different ethnic groups is not available, and it is vital that the next Three-Yearly Review be used to obtain it. However, such research as has been done suggests that ethnic minority children may be overrepresented in certain types of preschool care or education. For instance, in a study that is admittedly not very recent, it emerged that black children were disproportionately represented in social services day nurseries compared with their numbers in the local population (Van der Eyken, 1984). A more recent examination of day care services for children by the OPCS on behalf of the Department of Health found that:

● Nearly twice as many (41%) Asian or Oriental children did not use any services compared with children from other ethnic groups. West Indian or African children were more likely to be cared for by non-relatives than any other group; although they were less likely to be cared for by grandparents than white children, they were more likely than white children to be looked after by other relatives (OPCS, 1994).

- West Indian or African children were more than twice as likely (16%) to use day nurseries as white children (7%) (OPCS, 1994).

- 22% of white children attended sessional playgroups compared with 9% of Asian and Oriental children and 5% of West Indian and African children (OPCS, 1994).

- A greater percentage of West Indian or African children (22%) and Asian or Oriental children (20%) attended nursery school or class than white children (14%) (OPCS, 1994).

- 11% of West Indian or African children were looked after by a registered childminder compared with 6% of white children and 2% of Asian and Oriental children (OPCS, 1994).

Disparities between ethnic groups are not necessarily a sign of racial discrimination, but they do give legitimate cause for concern and require explanation. Data should therefore be monitored and analysed (as required by the Guidance to the Children Act) both at local authority and individual service level, to see whether any disparities can be explained by non-racial factors, before making assumptions about discrimination.

The best ways of preventing discrimination are to ensure that access to early childhood services is based on clear and objective admission and referral criteria; that information about the different services is readily available, in languages other than English where necessary; and that catchment areas do not unjustifiably exclude areas of ethnic minority residence.

THE EXPERIENCES OF YOUNG CHILDREN AND RACIAL EQUALITY

All young children should be encouraged to hold positive attitudes towards themselves and others. Unfortunately, racial prejudice is still widespread in our society. As soon as young children begin to learn anything, they can pick up the prejudices from the world around them. By the time they enter primary school, some children may be well on the road to believing that they are superior to others because of the colour of their skin, or the language they speak or the way they dress (Milner, 1983). What is learned about 'race' in these early years can decisively shape people's attitudes and behaviour later in life, and potentially damage and disadvantage children from other racial groups.

Most people do not see themselves as racially prejudiced and would not wish to be associated with openly racist views or behaviour. But many do not realise how readily children pick up unspoken assumptions and attitudes. Everyone involved in early childhood education and care throughout the country has a responsibility to see that this does not happen. In some areas, the emphasis may be on helping ethnic minority children develop a positive view of themselves, in others on helping all children to grow up with a positive view of others. Everywhere, though, the principle of multicultural, anti-racist education for early learners should be a priority for all.

A narrow environment which denies children the opportunity to develop positive attitudes towards others, and towards other ways of life, is harmful to all. Being proud of one's culture is not the same as thinking it is superior to others. The task of those who work with young children is to give all children the ability to live their lives to the full and to function effectively in society. Teachers and carers need to be able to recognise and eliminate racial discrimination in the provision of care and learning for the very young; know how to deal with prejudice; and how to make the most of every child's motivation by making them feel fully included, both as individuals and as children from different ethnic backgrounds.

Diversity adds value to society, and a learning environment which ignores this and reflects only one cultural perspective puts all children at a disadvantage. Reflecting Britain's multicultural society, and valuing all people equally, are professional goals that should be shared by everyone who cares for young children.

Differences

Treating people equally does not mean treating them all in the same way. Every child is unique, and this should be taken into account when meeting his or her needs.

There is nothing wrong in talking about the differences between children, as long as the differences are discussed positively, and seen as a source of enjoyment rather than disparagement, dislike or abuse (Derman-Sparks et al, 1989). Indeed, differences need to be acknowledged if children are not to feel that important aspects of themselves are being disregarded or ignored.

Staff working with very young children need to know how to answer questions about racial and cultural differences. Questions such as 'Why am I black?' or 'Why is she black?' should not be avoided, but answered clearly, factually, and simply, at a level suitable for a young child. If staff do not know the answers, they should say so openly, and seek help from others in providing a response as soon as possible.

Language and culture are integral to a child's sense of identity.

Positive support for the language a child uses at home actually strengthens the framework for learning English, and improves overall performance. All children should be helped to understand that English is but one among many languages and that the ability to communicate in more than one language is a strength, not a weakness.

Learning resources

Books, dolls, jigsaws, posters, games, and other toys should be a mirror to the multiethnic society we live in, and should be chosen carefully (Dixon, 1989; WGARCR, 1995a, 1995b, 1995c). Good racial equality practice has simply added an extra dimension to the selection criteria. The way these resources are used in play and learning can be as important as the objects themselves, and should be included in the general professional training all staff receive.

Examples

- Nurseries should make sure their dolls represent a variety of physical characteristics, skin tones and hair textures.

- Parents of children at the nursery can be asked to bring in for 'dressing up' clothes which are traditionally worn by different ethnic groups living in Britain today.

- Foodstuffs used to teach children to weigh and calculate should be drawn from a variety of cultures and cuisines. Children should also be made to understand that the use of chopsticks, fingers or cutlery are merely different ways of eating and that no one way is better or more 'proper' than another.

Teachers and carers should encourage *all* children, whatever their ethnic background, to take part in these activities, and share their home cultures with others.

Childrearing practices

Where there is an emphasis on developmental 'stages', care should be taken to avoid making ethnocentric judgements that might lead to some children being labelled as 'culturally deprived', for example because they do not play with manufactured toys bought from a toy shop. The norms and criteria used to assess developmental progress should always be relevant and objective, so that staff do not wrongly conclude that children who have been brought up within different childrearing traditions are falling behind.

When children are picked up from the nursery by various relatives, this is sometimes criticised as failing to give the child a proper sense of consistency or security. What is not recognised is that the children may come from families where different members, whom they fully trust, look after them and share responsibility for meeting them at the end of the day.

There is no single 'best' way to bring up a child, and there are as many differences in childrearing practices among both white and ethnic minority families as there are between them.

Stereotypes

The expectations which teachers and others have of a child's potential tend to be self-fulfilling. Stereotyping can have serious, long-term consequences, especially if a stereotype about a particular group results in low expectations of intellectual performance. For example, if the stereotype of a particular ethnic group is that its members lack the ability to concentrate, children from this group may be allowed to wander off from a particular task and not be encouraged to concentrate and develop various learning skills in the same way as the other children. Most damagingly, children from the ethnic group in question may adapt their behaviour to fulfil this expectation. Faced with unfamiliar situations, teachers and carers should make sure that they do not make unjustified assumptions that impede understanding and respect.

The growth of ethnic minority parents' groups and many supplementary schools and mother tongue classes indicates that ethnic minority parents are strongly committed to education in general and to their own children's academic progress in particular. Despite the social and economic disadvantages which many ethnic minority families experience, there is evidence that they are more committed to their children's formal education than white families (Tizard et al, 1988). Teachers and carers should recognise the role they can play in challenging and eliminating harmful stereotypes. Strategies for involving parents in the care and education of children will assist this process.

Racial harassment

Racial harassment, a form of behaviour which is offensive or hurtful to others on racial grounds, is often not taken seriously where young children are concerned. Laughing at someone's hair, or their clothes or their accent, or the colour of their skin, or because they speak in another language, can be deeply hurtful. Children are unlikely to reach their full potential if they have to contend with racial harassment. All instances of harassment, whether they occur at the nursery or playgroup or on the way to or from home, should be taken seriously. Incidents can range from 'jokes' and gibes about a child's personal appearance or culture to racist graffiti, and physical attacks.

Teachers and carers should be sensitive to the way children interact and relate to each other. All incidents of racial harassment should be recorded and dealt with as part of a comprehensive monitoring strategy for the service. Staff also need to know how to deal with incidents of racist abuse or behaviour; children who suffer from such harassment should be strongly supported, while those responsible for it need sensitive counselling and the opportunity to reflect on their actions in an atmosphere of support for themselves personally while it is clearly and firmly explained that their behaviour is unacceptable.

Attainment

It is now well-established that children's future attainment levels depend on a variety of factors, including the relationships they have with their carers and teachers. Evidence shows that black boys, in particular, appear to have the least contact with teachers (Tizard et al, 1988). Teachers and carers of the under-fives should ensure, through practice and observation, that all children have equal access to the development of learning skills, and to the care and attention of the adults around them.

Assessment

Before using formalised tests, it is worth considering their functions. Why is the information needed? Would more useful information be obtained through sensitive observation of child ren's spontaneous behaviour? (Drummond et al, 1992).

Those responsible for young children and babies need to consider whether any assessment takes account of a child's first language, and whether the assessment is culturally biased. While it is almost impossible to devise 'culture-free' tests, some tests have been standardised on samples of white middle-class child ren, and the resulting 'norms' may be inappropriate for ethnic minority children, among others. Particular care needs to be taken when assessing children's behaviour or development, or when making decisions about a child's needs, to avoid stereotyping and unnecessary subjectivity.

Some children who speak English at the nursery or playgroup may be bilingual (or even multilingual). When assessing a child's language development, it should be recognised that a child may be able to name something in his or her home language, but not yet in English. Language development tests should be based on the assumption that learning to be bilingual is something positive. In order that a test be as objective as possible, there is a case for it to be administered in the child's home language, and by someone familiar with, and sympathetic to, the child's cultural background.

Special educational needs

The *Code of Practice on the Identification and Assessment of Special Educational Needs* (DFE, 1994), which has a special section on under-fives, states that children with a learning difficulty or developmental delay whose parents do not have English as a first language may be particularly disadvantaged if any special educational needs are not identified at the earliest possible stage. It states that LEAs should ensure that parents are provided with interpreters and translated information and that bilingual support staff should be available to help. Schools should also have information in a range of relevant languages.

All the tests used must, ideally, be as culturally unbiased as possible, and standardised for all the relevant ethnic groups. With regard to those making the assessment, as well as the parent's 'named person', the LEA should take particular care to ensure that they reflect the child's linguistic, cultural and community background. They should also stress that, when considering assessment or a statement, parents may be accompanied by a friend who understands the child's needs. Wherever possible, oral interviews with parents should be conducted in their first language. Staff in early childhood services play a critical role in helping to identify special needs. Stereotypes should not be allowed to interfere with this process.

EQUAL ACCESS TO EARLY CHILDHOOD PROVISION

The wide variety of provision (local authority, statutory, voluntary and private sector) which exists at present is not the result of careful and sensitive planning to provide flexible choices. This has made it particularly difficult to assess whether the service overall is delivering equality of opportunity for all children and their families. Many authorities have taken significant steps towards better planning of early years services. The Children Act provides a framework for a coordinated early years management structure at a local level. Examples include combining education and day care services under one management structure, usually that of the education department; moving towards an integrated approach, (although not necessarily with an integrated management structure) by developing a common early years policy and common strategy for its implementation; and developing a common training strategy in which educators in all sectors can participate.

Admissions

While the registration of non-LEA provision by social services departments should have removed racially discriminatory admission arrangements, a re-examination of the admissions operations for all oversubscribed nurseries (including LEA nurseries) and playgroups may reveal that some of them are unintentionally excluding particular racial groups disproportionately.

Example

- Families who have only recently arrived in Britain and have little knowledge of English may be less likely than others to put their children's names on a waiting list run on a first-come, first-served basis, because they are less familiar with the 'system' of early childhood services and do not know people who could advise them. Allocating places in this way may therefore disadvantage them.

In Britain, unlike most other countries of the European Union, there is a severe shortage of childcare and education provision overall. Offers of places should therefore be based on objective selection criteria, open to public scrutiny and carefully monitored and analysed. This may also help to ensure that any ethnic differences in the composition of morning and afternoon nursery sessions are the result of personal preferences and not because some parents are, in effect, being offered less choice on racial grounds (for examples of indirect discrimination in admissions, see CRE, 1992a). Waiting lists should be used to record the names and details of potential applicants, instead of being used as a basis for allocation. Places should then be allocated, from these names, using objective selection criteria, as described above.

Local patterns

Local audits of the use of early childhood provision, classified by ethnic group, need to be conducted to establish an ethnic profile of the families using each type of service, and of staff in each service, and to see whether any distinctive patterns emerge. These can then be analysed, and appropriate action taken to redress any less favourable treatment to certain groups. The Three-Yearly Review required by the Children Act should address these issues (see p 27). It is one opportunity for parents to be involved in the service and to identify the support they need.

Examples

- More flexible opening hours may attract a more varied clientele.

- Information, or advertisements, targeted at places used by ethnic minority groups, and in languages other than English, may remove barriers to access for certain minority groups.

Group day care

Ethnic monitoring should cover the following areas: all applicants and successful applicants for places; current enrolments; all staff; management committees; and governing bodies. The monitoring may reveal a pattern of exclusion for particular ethnic minority groups, in some or all areas, and make clear who the service is, in practice, being provided for. The monitoring and subsequent reviews of policies and procedures to explain any disparities will also show how decisions are made, and by whom, and whether the service may be unlawfully discriminating against particular ethnic groups.

Childminders

Chapter one highlights the ambiguity of a childminder's legal obligations. The tripartite relationship between local authority, registered minder and parent is a complex one which is not clearly addressed by the Race Relations Act.

Childminding is a widely-used and valued option for many parents, particularly working parents for whom the hours on offer in playgroups and nurseries simply do not cover their basic needs, even if they would prefer their child to attend one. Nurseries and playgroups rarely have places for children under two or three. Childminding is a positive choice for an increasing number of parents who prefer their children to spend most of their day in a home environment, getting individual attention, supplemented by playgroup or nursery attendance for group experience, as they get older.

However, just because large numbers of ethnic minority families already use childminders, this does not mean that equality of opportunity and access are not issues. Several questions need to be answered: Is the choice of minders wide enough? Does the list of local registered minders reflect the ethnic composition of the area? What criteria do the local authority use when deciding to register or deregister childminders? Are minders allowed to specify which groups of children they will take?

This is an area where the Race Relations Act and the Children Act clearly overlap, and it would be useful to examine the duties a local authority has under each of these laws.

The Race Relations Act

- Local authorities have a duty to make appropriate arrangements to eliminate unlawful racial discrimination and to promote equality of opportunity between people from different racial groups (Section 71). This will apply to the services they provide for registering childminders and helping parents find suitable childminders for their children.

- If a childminder attempts to put pressure on a registration officer or day care adviser not to refer children from a particular racial group, the officer can:

  - Ask the CRE to pursue the matter under Section 31 (pressure to discriminate) on the grounds that, by complying with such pressure the officer or adviser will be in breach of Sections 71 and 20 (provision of services). Although this may be the only course of action in some circumstances, it might be seen as a rather heavy-handed response.

  - Comply with the pressure and only refer children from the racial group requested. This would be unlawful.

- Ignore the pressure altogether and continue to refer children from all racial groups. Although the officer or adviser would be complying with the letter of the law, they would not be dealing with the childminder and would be allowing parents to visit the childminder in the knowledge that their child is likely to be refused a place on racial grounds. The registration officer or day care adviser would be colluding with discrimination.

- The Commission and the NCMA believe that such childminders are unsuitable to care for any child.

- It is not just local authority staff who would be liable under the law if they yielded to pressure from a childminder to discriminate on racial grounds. Liability under the law applies equally to the following agencies, which in fact make more placements than local authorities:

  - private agencies helping parents to find childcare

  - employer-resourced childminding networks

  - local childminding groups' vacancy schemes

  - the National Childminding Association's resource and referral scheme.

The Children Act

The Children Act clarifies the situation in several ways:

- Where a registered childminder fails to take account of a child's religious persuasion, racial origin, cultural and linguistic background, the Children Act allows their registration to be cancelled.

- The Guidance accompanying the Act makes it clear that points to be considered in determining whether a person is fit to care for children (and should be registered) include knowledge of multicultural issues and 'a commitment and knowledge to treat all children as individuals and with equal concern'.

Local authorities are justified, therefore, in addressing this area through their registration criteria.

● It would be lawful for a local authority, or any other agency, to help match parents with childminders if the parents have specific requirements concerning their child's welfare and personal needs.

Examples

● The parent of a very young child may prefer a childminder who speaks the language used in the child's home.

● A parent may have specific dietary requirements for a child and expect the childminder to be able to accommodate these, for example, halal meat or vegetarian dishes.

By identifying the specific skills and qualifications that childminders offer, local authorities can help families find childminders who can meet their children's cultural, religious and linguistic needs.

In-service support and training

Support and training on equality of opportunity and anti-discriminatory practice, taking account of all the issues raised in this guide, should be available to everyone who works with young children. Individual training needs should be identified as part of a comprehensive programme of in-service support at all levels and in all types of organisation: statutory, private and voluntary. Training should be integrated with practice.

In-service training in this field should be sensitive to the reluctance shown by some people to consider the issues, while not losing sight of the main objective of the course. It is always possible to find common aims, for example that all children should learn to care about each other, and these shared goals can be used to discuss what they involve, and how they can be translated into practice. Change takes time and, like developing an equal opportunity policy, the process is best undertaken over a long period, with many opportunities for discussion. At the same time, a balance has to be struck which takes account of the unquestionable right of children not to be subjected to discrimination, prejudice or harassment.

Resources are also needed on a continuous basis, and include practical guidance on good multicultural and anti-racist practice in childcare and education. Useful organisations are listed at the end of this booklet. The references and further reading suggested at the end of this booklet list resources for in-service training and support.

In a few areas, local support groups have been set up to consider policy and practice and to discuss particular concerns. This has proved to be an effective way of examining issues in depth.

TRAINING, EDUCATION AND QUALIFICATIONS FOR WORK WITH YOUNG CHILDREN

The achievement of equal opportunity and racial equality in early years services depends on the skills, knowledge and attitudes of those involved. These skills cannot be taken for granted, and should be specifically addressed in all areas of work with young children: employment, education and training.

In addition to its *Code of Practice... in Employment* (CRE, 1984), the CRE has published guidance on positive action (CRE, 1991b).

Recruitment and selection

Each stage of the recruitment and selection process, for potential students as well as employees, needs to be scrutinised, to determine whether ethnic minority applicants are being discriminated against, and whether the procedures being used are potentially discriminatory.

With few exceptions (such as the specific entry requirements laid down by the DFEE with regard to entry to initial teacher education, Bachelor of Education and Postgraduate Certificate of Education courses), similar issues of recruitment and selection apply to courses in higher and further education institutions, and the following action should be taken or considered to ensure equality of opportunity:

- targeting areas or schools which have large numbers of ethnic minority pupils but which yield few applications

- determining areas of work in early childhood education and care where particular ethnic groups are underrepresented, and organising courses specifically for those groups, as permitted under Section 37 of the Race Relations Act (see page 18)

- producing information and literature on: the service's policies on equal opportunity and racial harassment; its plans for implementing them; the way student placements and school experience are organised; and the selection process, including the criteria for selection

- advertising widely

- ensuring that no entry requirement has an unjustifiable discriminatory impact on particular racial groups, for example, asking for specific qualifications or experience

- using a variety of methods for assessing qualifications

- training interviewers on equal opportunity principles (Darling and Hedge, 1992)

- monitoring key stages in the recruitment and selection process by ethnic group

- examining any factors in the recruitment and selection process which appear to be racially discriminatory, and dealing with any unlawful discrimination found.

The advent of National Vocational Qualifications in England, Wales and Northern Ireland, and Scottish Vocational Qualifications in Scotland, are welcome in that the system is based on open access to assessment. There are no entry requirements. Any candidate who is competent to the occupational standards can register for assessment, no matter how that competence has been developed (through formal training, informal learning, experience or personal development). The awarding bodies' criteria for approval of assessment centres include written equal opportunity policies and implementation strategies. All assessors for NVQ under the Care Sector Consortium must have anti-discrimination training. Candidates must not be denied access to assessment, nor their competence be less favourably assessed because of their ethnic background. This is reinforced by appeals procedures. Candidates put forward by employers for such assessment should be monitored by ethnic group.

The steps listed above are similar to those required when recruiting and selecting for employment in childcare or education. The criteria listed in the person specification as being necessary for the work that is to be done should not discriminate unlawfully against particular racial groups; and may include knowledge of, and commitment to, racial equality.

Practices which can discriminate against potential ethnic minority students have been uncovered in various areas of education. For example, a survey by the CRE in 1986 of colleges offering NNEB qualifications found a complete absence of national standards or criteria governing access to such courses. However, the majority of childcare awarding bodies have now incorporated equal opportunities principles into their practice. Further specific examples of good practice in recruitment and selection are listed below.

Methods of recruitment and advertising

- If there are not many ethnic minority applicants, consult the local communities to establish the reasons for this.

- Advertise in the ethnic minority press, and produce information about the course in the languages used locally. Offer support to develop written and oral skills in English.

- Ensure that, wherever possible, the prospectus reflects the ethnic composition of the local community.

The application form

- Explain why you are asking for information about applicants' ethnic origins, and say how the information will and will not be used.

- Do not ask for applicants' 'Christian' name; 'name' and 'first name' are more likely to be understood by all applicants.

- Do not ask for photographs, as people are likely to fear that they will be used to discriminate against them.

- Do not ask unnecessary, and possibly unlawful, questions about nationality, country of birth and immigration status. If you need to identify applicants who are liable for overseas students' fees, this can be done separately later at the enrolment stage.

Entry requirements

- Make sure that all specified entry requirements are necessary for the work or training in question

- Specify that students must be willing to accept all children whatever their racial group, and have a positive interest in the care and education of young children in a multiracial society.

- Try not to use criteria that may be subjective and culturally loaded; for example 'appropriate temperament', 'suitable personality' 'good dress sense'.

Entrance tests

- Ensure, as far as possible, that any tests used are not culturally biased. All tests should be validated for all ethnic groups.

References

- Invite referees for an applicant to comment against a set of agreed selection criteria which are objectively important for the work or training.

Interviews

- Provide applicants, in advance, with details of the interview assessment procedures.

- Interviewers should be aware of how stereotyping can influence decision-making, particularly if the first language of the interviewee is not the same as that of the panel.

- Interviewers should ensure that assessment is not based on non-verbal signals or body language. For example, in many cultures it is considered disrespectful to make direct eye contact with someone in a position of authority.

- Panels should make every effort to include people from ethnic minority groups, while guarding against using them in a tokenistic way; for example by expecting them to ask the questions related to equal opportunities.

- Interviews should be conducted against agreed, non-discriminatory, objective criteria. These should include a positive commitment to equality of opportunity and the elimination of racial discrimination.

Other education and training issues

The need to address equal opportunity issues does not end once students are accepted for the course. What, and how, they are taught is central to their ability to work in a multiracial society and to deliver a service that meets the needs of all the children they may teach, or care for, during their career.

Education and training for work with young children includes infant and nursery teacher education, training for nursery nurses, health visitors, social workers, playgroup staff and childminders, and school-based childcare courses. Staff need to be selected who are able to provide the education and training in a way that follows the guidance described in this booklet.

Curriculum

The issues raised in this booklet should be integral to the course, not added on as an extra.

Good practice suggestions

- Examine learning resources, including child development text books (WGARCR, 1991).

- Prepare students to recognise signs of prejudice or discrimination and deal with them in a positive way. These might range from unreasonably excluding a child from a play activity to verbal and physical attacks.

- Prepare students to discuss physical and cultural differences with children in positive terms.

- Ensure that students know why the question of racial equality is relevant in Britain today.

- Plan regular sessions to discuss what racial equality means in terms of people's attitudes and behaviour.

Student placements

Racial harassment is an issue that affects both the institution itself and school and nursery placements or practice. Placements should therefore be selected in the light of the issues raised in this booklet. Work experience is best acquired where the nursery or playgroup has an effective and well planned equal opportunities policy. A contract between the institution, the student and the placement to ensure equality of treatment provides a basis for student confidence and support within a defined framework. The experiences of many ethnic minority students in initial teacher education provides little ground for complacency (see, for instance, research reported in Siraj-Blatchford, 1991).

Examination boards and validation/accreditation bodies

Examination boards and validation and accreditation bodies need to establish assessment criteria which include equal opportunities considerations.

Boards need to ensure that their examinations and assessment procedures do not discriminate unlawfully on racial grounds.

Examples of good practice

● Use candidate numbers instead of names as far as possible throughout the examination and assessment procedure.

● Train examiners and assessors in equal opportunity procedures.

● In oral examinations, use standardised questions and recording mechanisms. Where possible, examine in teams.

● Have two examiners marking papers (double marking).

● Use external examiners to ensure standardisation and, to be objective, use mediators in determining attainment levels.

● Introduce an independent appeals procedure.

PRACTICAL POLICY MAKING

Many organisations are involved in some way with young children: local authorities, health authorities, voluntary and private sector organisations, research bodies, examination boards, validating bodies, training organisations, consultants, professional bodies, learning materials manufacturers, and publishers, and, most immediately of all, early childhood services.

A policy for equality – which is much more than a statement about being an equal opportunities employer – is the starting point for all organisations in providing a service based on equality of opportunity and the elimination of unlawful racial discrimination.

In areas of Britain where there are few people from ethnic minorities, it is important to be clear why an equal opportunities policy is necessary. Children need to learn to respect people different from themselves. Quite apart from the fact that racial prejudice is damaging to all children, there are objective reasons too. They may move to live and work in more ethnically diverse surroundings, or they may take up jobs that have important consequences for people from ethnic minorities, such as the immigration service. It is vital that they have a positive outlook and understanding of our multicultural society.

While each organisation will develop a policy that suits its particular needs, there are certain principles of good practice that apply to all:

- wide discussion and consultation throughout the organisation about what an equal opportunities policy means, and what its short- and long-term objectives should be

- ongoing consultation with relevant groups and individuals

outside the organisation. For example, local communities, governors, managers, parents, and groups concerned with equal opportunity issues (including those listed on page 77)

- examination of the organisation's structures, practices and procedures in all areas of its work, and particularly those that involve decision-making, in order to identify the scope of the policy

- consideration, in advance, of how to avoid marginalising the policy and how to enlist the support of employees at all levels in implementing it. This is crucial, and is time well-spent in terms of the policy's long-term success.

The next step, once the policy has been agreed, will be to develop an action plan covering all of the following:

- commitment of resources to stop any discrimination revealed through ethnic monitoring and analysis

- collection throughout the organisation of ethnic data on employment, service delivery, and racial harassment

- monitoring, evaluation and continuous review of data and progress, to ensure that the policy is being implemented at every level of decision-making

- a clear framework for monitoring and analysing incidents of racial harassment, including procedures for reporting them

- a timetable for action

- procedures for rectifying any inequalities or discrimination found

- clearly defined responsibility for policy implementation at the highest level and for action at every level

- regular reviews of the policy, practices and procedures, to ensure their effective implementation.

Finally, given the considerable changes in the private sector, local authorities will need to develop guidelines of good practice for all organisations concerned with young children, so that the services they provide are properly coordinated.

CHECKLIST FOR ACTION

If you are a parent, a childminder, a health visitor, a social worker, a teacher, a carer, a nursery nurse, a playgroup leader, a member of staff in a creche, playbus or parent and toddler group, a trainer, an adviser or an employer, or if you are responsible for developing policy for a local authority or a private or voluntary sector organisation, you should go through the following questions. Some of the questions will apply to everyone, others are relevant only to some groups.

The checklist is not an exhaustive list of areas for action, but if you are interested in equality of opportunity and wish to improve the service you are involved with, you should answer the following questions:

- How does the Race Relations Act apply to the particular type of early childhood service you are involved with?

- Do you have copies of the CRE's Codes of Practice in employment and in education, and copies of the CRE's racial equality standards in employment and in local government, *Racial Equality Means Business*, and *Racial Equality means Quality*?

- What steps do you take to ensure that your registration and inspection procedures for childminders and day care providers take account of the 'race' implications of the Children Act? In particular, have you developed criteria for evaluating standards of care with respect to racial equality issues?

- Do you provide pre-registration training on childcare and education with respect to racial equality issues?

- Do you offer ongoing support and in-service training for registered childminders, day care providers and early years teachers and carers on racial equality issues?

- What steps have you taken to develop local networks for sharing ideas and information on racial equality issues?

- Do you ensure that both education and social services departments work together to provide an early years service based on principles of equality of opportunity.

- Do you make sure that the Three-Yearly Review collects ethnic information on all aspects of under-eights services – for example who goes where, and who applies; who works where, and who applies – and then analyse the data and examine any disparities between nurseries and playgroups, taking account of the ethnic composition of the local community.

- Does your admissions policy exclude any racial group or reduce their chances of a place, however unintentionally?

- Does your learning material and equipment reflect the cultures, faiths and languages of the diverse ethnic groups living in Britain today?

- What steps have you taken to ensure that your staff and volunteers reflect the ethnic composition of the local area?

- Do you make sure that information about early childhood services is widely available, and in languages other than English?

- Do you understand what 'positive action' means, and what steps can be taken under the Race Relations Act?

- Are you aware of the ways in which racial stereotyping can affect the learning of very young children, whatever their ethnic background?

- Do you provide equal opportunities training for those who sit on selection panels?

- Does your organisation have a policy on racial harassment, perhaps as a specific element of a policy on behaviour? Is ethnic data collected and analysed on such incidents? What procedures are there for reporting incidents?

- Does your organisation have an equal opportunities policy? If so, how is ethnic data monitored and analysed, and the information used to make sure the policy is effective?

- Does your organisation allocate adequate resources to realise its commitment to equality of opportunity and prevent racial discrimination?

REFERENCES

Amin, K, with Oppenheim, C (1992) *Poverty in Black and White: Deprivation and Ethnic Minorities.* Child Poverty Action Group, The Runnymede Trust.

Bartholomew, R, Hibbert, A, and Sidaway, J (1992) 'Lone parents and the labour market: Evidence from the Labour Force Survey' in *Employment Gazette,* November.

Commission for Racial Equality (1984) *Race Relations Code of Practice: For the elimination of racial discrimination and the promotion of equality of opportunity in employment.*

– (1986) *Teaching English as a Second Language: Report of a Formal Investigation in Calderdale Local Education Authority.*

– (1989) *Code of Practice for the Elimination of Racial Discrimination in Education.*

– (1991a) *Code of Practice for the Elimination of Racial Discrimination in Education (Scotland).*

– (1991b) *Positive Action and Equal Opportunity in Employment.*

– (1991c) *A Measure of Equality: monitoring and achieving racial equality in employment.*

– (1992a) *Secondary School Admissions: Report of a Formal Investigation into Hertfordshire County Council.*

– (1992b) *Ethnic Monitoring in Education.*

(1994) *Job advertisements and the Race Relations Act: A guide to Section 5 for advertisers and publishers*

– (1995a) *Racial Equality Means Business: A standard for racial equality for employers*

– (1995b) *Racial Equality Means Quality: A standard for racial equality for local government in England and Wales.* (A parallel standard for local government in Scotland is also available.)

– and Equal Opportunities Commission (1995c) *Further Education and Equality: A manager's manual.*

Darling, B, and Hedge, A (1992) *Fair Interviewing.* Trentham Books.

Department for Education (1994) *Code of Practice on the Identification and Assessment of Special Educational Needs.*

Department of Employment (1988) 'Labour Force Survey 1985, Unpublished Tables 1984-86: Averages', cited in *Caring for Children: Services and Policies for Childcare and Equal Opportunities in the United Kingdom.* Report by the European Commission's Childcare Network.

Derman-Sparks, L, and The ABC Task Force (1989) *Anti-Bias Curriculum: Tools for empowering young children.* National Association for the Education of Young Children, Washington, DC, USA (available from National Early Years Network, 77 Holloway Road, London N7 8JZ)

Dixon, B (1989) *Playing them False: A study of children's toys, games and puzzles.* Trentham Books.

Drummond, M J, Rouse, D, Pugh, G (1992) *Making Assessment work: Values and principles in assessing young children's learning.* NES Arnold. National Children's Bureau.

Equal Opportunities Commission (1994) *An Equal Start: Guidelines on equal treatment for the under eights.*

Her Majesty's Stationery Office (1991) *The Children Act 1989, Guidance and Regulations: Volume 2 Family Support, Day Care and Educational Provision for Young Children.* HMSO.

House of Commons, Education, Science & Arts Committee (1989) *Educational Provision for the Under Fives.* HMSO.

Jones, T (1993) *Britain's Ethnic Minorities: An analysis of the Labour Force Survey.* Policy Studies Institute.

Kumar, V (1993) *Poverty and Inequality in the UK: The effects on children.* National Children's Bureau.

Labour Force Survey (1989-91) Unpublished Tables.

London Research Centre (1994) *Homelessness in London*, Bulletin 4.

Macdonald, S (1991) *All Equal under the Act: a practical guide to the Children Act 1989 for social workers*. Race Equality Unit, National Institute for Social Work.

Milner, D (1983) *Children and Race: Ten years on*. Ward Lock Educational.

National Children's Bureau/Early Childhood Unit (1995) *With Equal Concern – training materials to ensure day care and educational provision for young children takes positive account of the 'religious persuasion, racial origin and cultural and linguistic background of each child' (Children Act 1989)*. This is closely related to the training pack, *Ensuring standards in the care of young children: registering and developing quality day care*, NCB/ECU (1991).

National Commission on Education (1993) *Learning to Succeed: A Radical Look at Education Today and a Strategy for the Future*. Heinemann.

National Curriculum Council (1990a) *Curriculum Guidance 3: The Whole Curriculum*.

–   (1990b) *Curriculum Guidance 8: Education for Citizenship*.

National Ethnic Minority Data Archive (1993a) *1991 Census Statistical Paper No 2*. University of Warwick.

–   (1993b) *1991 Census Statistical Paper No 4*. University of Warwick.

Office of Population Censuses and Surveys (OPCS), Social Survey Division (1994) *Day care services for children: a survey carried out on behalf of the Department of Health in 1990*, by Howard Meltzer, HMSO.

Runnymede Trust (1993) *Equality Assurance in Schools – quality, identity, society: a handbook for action planning and school effectiveness*. Trentham Books.

Siraj-Blatchford, I (1991) 'A study of Black Students' Perceptions of Racism' in *Initial Teacher Education. British Educational Research Journal*, vol 17 no 1.

Sylva, K, Siraj-Blatchford, I, and Johnson, S (1992) 'The impact of the UK National Curriculum on Pre-School Practice: Some "top-down" processes at work' in *International Journal of Early Childhood*, vol 24 no 1 pp 41-51.

Tizard, B, Blatchford, P, Burke, J, Farquhar, C, Plewis, I (1988) *Young children at School in the Inner City*. Lawrence Erlbaum Associates.

Trades Union Congress (1995a) *Black Workers and the Labour Market*, Black Workers Conference.

Trades Union Congress (1995b) *Black and Betrayed: A TUC report on black workers' experience of unemployment and low pay in 1994-95.*

Van der Eyken, W (1984) *Day Nurseries in Action*. Department of Child Health Research Unit, University of Bristol/DHSS.

Working Group Against Racism in Children's Resources (1991) *Guidelines: for the selection and evaluation of child development books.*

– (revised 1995a) *Guidelines: for the evaluation and selection of toys and other resources for children.*

– (1995b) *Guidelines and more selected titles for the evaluation and selection of children's picture books.*

– (1995c) *Resource list: anti-racist resources for the under eights and where to find them.*

FURTHER READING

Brown, C, Barnfield, J, Stone, M (1991) *Spanner in the Works: Education for racial equality and social justice in white schools.* Trentham Books.

Brooking, C, Foster, M, and Smith, S (1987) *Teaching for equality: Education resources on race and gender.* The Runnymede Trust.

Commission for Racial Equality (1988) *Learning in Terror: A survey of racial harassment in schools and colleges.*

Department of Education and Science (1990) *Starting with Quality: Report of the Committee of Inquiry into the Quality of the Educational Experience offered to three and four year olds.* HMSO.

Derman-Sparks, L, and The ABC Task Force (1989) *Anti-Bias Curriculum: Tools for empowering young children.* National Association for The Education of Young Children, Washington DC, USA (available from National Early Years Network, 77 Holloway Road, London N7 8JZ)

Early Years Trainers Anti-racist Network (1991) *Selecting for equality.* (Available from EYTARN, PO Box 1870, London N12 8JQ).

– (1992) *Learning by doing: The anti-racist way.*

– (1993) *Equality in Practice.*

– (1993) *Racism: The white agenda.*

– (revised 1995) *All our children: a guide for those who care.* Commissioned by the BBC.

– (1995) *Best of both worlds: celebrating mixed parentage.*

– (1995) *Partnership with parents: an anti-discriminatory approach.*

European Commission's Childcare Network (1988) *Caring for Children: Services and policies for childcare and equal opportunities in the United Kingdom.* (Available from Commission of the European Communities, 8 Storey's Gate, London SW1 2AT).

Gregory, E, and Kelly, C (1992) *Bilingualism and Assessment in Assessment in Early Childhood Education, ed by* G Blenkin and A V Kelly. Paul Chapman Publishing.

Joseph, C, Lane, J, and Sharma, S (1994) 'No Equality, No Quality' in Moss, P, and Pence, A (eds) *Valuing Quality in Early Childhood Services: new approaches to defining quality,* Paul Chapman Publishing Ltd.

Lane, J (1989) 'The Playgroup/Nursery' in M Cole (ed), *Education for Equality: Some guidelines for good practice.* Routledge.

– (1990) 'Sticks and Carrots: Using the Race Relations Act to remove bad practice and the Children Act to promote good practice' in *Local Government Policy Making,* vol 1 no 3 (December).

– (1992) 'The 1989 Children Act: A framework for racial equality in children's day care/education' in *Early Years,* vol 12 no 2 (spring).

– (1993) 'What role has the law played in getting rid of racism in the lives of children?' in Pugh (ed) *30 years of Change for Children.* National Children's Bureau.

McFarlane, C (1986) *Hidden Messages: Activities for exploring bias.* (Available from Development Education Centre, Gillette Centre. Selly Oak College, Bristol Road, Birmingham B29 6LQ).

National Childminding Association (1991) *Setting the Standards; guidelines on good practice in registering childminders.*

– (1992) *Childminder Factfile/Handbook.*

– (1993) *Equal Opportunities in childminding: a guide to training and resource materials for tutors.* With the assistance of Bedfordshire County Council, Equal Opportunities Committee.

National Children's Bureau/Early Childhood Unit (1991) *Ensuring standards in the care of young children: registering and developing quality day care.*

– (1991) *Young children in group day care: Guidelines for good practice.* Compiled by L Cowley.

National Association of Toy and Leisure Libraries (1989) *Play For All: A booklet to help toy librarians, teachers and playgroup workers reflect the pluralist nature of British society.*

O'Hagan, M, Smith, M (1993) *Special Issues in Child Care: a comprehensive NVQ-linked textbook.* Balliere Tindall.

Pre-school Learning Alliance, Guidelines (1990) *Good practice for parent and toddler playgroups.*

– (1991) *Equal Chances: Eliminating discrimination and ensuring equality in playgroups.*

– (1993) *Good practice for sessional playgroups.*

– (1993) *Good practice for full and extended day care playgroups.*

Save the Children (1993) *Equality: a basis for good practice.*

Siraj-Blatchford, I (1994) *The Early Years: laying the foundations for racial equality.* Trentham Books

Troyna, B, and Hatcher, R (1992) *Racism in Children's Lives: A Study of Mainly-White Primary Schools.* Routledge, in association with the National Children's Bureau.

Wright, C (1992) *Race Relations in the Primary School.* David Fulton Publishers.

Other relevant CRE publications

A Measure of Equality: Monitoring and achieving racial equality in employment (1991).

Ethnic Monitoring in Education (1992).

Job Advertisements and the Race Relations Act: A guide to Section 5 for advertisers and publishers (1994).

Lessons of the law: a casebook of racial discrimination in education (1992).

No Room for Racism (1994). Written for 8-12 year-olds as a back-up to the Children's BBC series on racism, *Dynamite.*

Schools of Faith: Religious schools in a multicultural society (1990).

Set to Fail? Ethnic minority pupils in secondary education (1992).

Special Needs in Education: Recommendations for good practice (forthcoming).

Training: The implementation of equal opportunities at work, Vols I and II (1987).

Why Keep Ethnic Records? (Revised edition 1991).

A current CRE catalogue is available from CRE Distribution Services, Elliot House, 10/12 Allington Street, London SW1E 5EH. Please send a stamped and self-addressed A5-size envelope.

USEFUL ORGANISATIONS

Access to Information on Multi-cultural Education Resources (AIMER)
Reading and Language Information Centre
University of Reading
Bulmershe Court, Earley
Reading RG6 1HY
☎ 01734 875123 Ext 4871

AIMER is a database project which offers students, teachers, advisers and others information on multicultural, antiracist teaching materials. In addition to a postal inquiry service, AIMER publishes resource lists on a wide range of topics including 'Games, Sports and Toys'. A publication list is available on request.

Afro-Caribbean Education Resource Project (ACER)
Wyvil School
Wyvil Road
London SW8 2TJ
☎ 0171 627 2662

ACER develops anti-racist and multicultural learning materials for use in schools (including nursery schools).

Anti-Racist Teacher Education Network (ARTEN)
c/o Samidha Garg
28 Shendish Edge
London Road
Apsley
Hemel Hempstead
Herts HP3 9SZ

ARTEN is a nationwide network committed to improving the quality of teacher education for the benefit of staff, students and children.

Black Childcare Network

c/o Hearsay
17 Brownhill Road
Catford London SE6 2EG
☎ 0181 697 2152

Black Childcare Network promotes anti-racist childcare policies and practice.

Children in Scotland

Princes House
5 Shandwick Place
Edinburgh EH2 4RG
☎ 0131 228 8484

This is a sister organisation of the National Children's Bureau and provides a range of information about children's services.

Children in Wales

7 Cleeve House
Lambourne Crescent
Cardiff CF4 5GJ
☎ 01222 761177

This is a sister organisation of the National Children's Bureau and provides a range of information about children's services.

Clybiau Plant Cymru

Ty Olfield
Llantrisant Road
Llandaff
Cardiff CF5 2YT
☎ 01222 563594

This is a Welsh equivalent of Kids' Club Network, working in partnership with it.

Daycare Trust
Wesley House
4 Wild Court
London WC2B 5AU
☎ 0171 405 5617/8

The Trust provides information and advise about childcare services for parents, professionals and providers.

Equality Learning Centre
Save the Children
London Voluntary Sector Resource Centre
356 Holloway Road
London N7 6PA
☎ 0171 700 8127

Equality Learning Centre has been set up to support professional development and provide information, reference and resource facilities, publications and training for early years workers.

Early Years Trainers Anti-Racist Network (EYTARN)
P O Box 1870
London N12 8JQ
☎ 0181 446 7056

EYTARN is a nationwide network of people working to encourage anti-racist practices in the education and care of young children.

Kids' Clubs Network
Bellerive House
3 Muirfield Crescent
London E14 9SZ
☎ 0171 512 2112

KCN is the recognised authority on out-of-school care. It currently includes 600 kids' clubs in the UK.

Mudiad Ysgolion Meithrin (National Association of Welsh Language Playgroups)
> 145 Albany Road
> Cardiff CF2 3NT
> ☎ 01222 485510

MYM aims to provide the opportunity for pre-school play activities, using the Welsh language, for all children in Wales who want it.

Multicultural Resource Centres
Many LEAs have multi-cultural resource centres. See phone book for the address of your LEA.

National Childcare Campaign (NCCC)
> Wesley House
> 4 Wild Court
> London WC2B 5AU
> ☎ 0171 405 5617/8

NCCC is an advocacy organisation which promotes childcare issues nationally and locally.

National Childminding Association (NCMA)
> 8 Masons Hill
> Bromley BR2 9EY
> ☎ 0181 464 6164

NCMA exists to promote childminding as a quality childcare service. Its primary purpose is to advise childminders, parents, employers and central and local government on best practice in childminding and how to achieve this.

National Childminding Association in Wales

Offices 4 and 5
The Lighthouse Business Park
Bastion Road
Prestatyn
Clywd LL19 7ND
☎ 01745 852995

NCMAW promotes services and provision for childminders, children and their parents. It promotes childminding as a quality family day care provision.

National Children's Bureau

Early Childhood Unit
8 Wakley Street
London EC1V 7QE
☎ 0171 843 6000

The Early Childhood Unit of the National Children's Bureau can provide a list of literature on equality of opportunity and anti-racist childcare/education organisation and practice. Please send a stamped and addressed envelope. There are sister organisations in Scotland and Wales, Children in Scotland and Children in Wales, listed separately.

National Council of Voluntary Child Care Organisations (NCVCCO)

Unit 4
Pride Court
80/82 White Lion Street
London N1 9PF
☎ 0171 833 3319

NCVCCO is a group of voluntary organisations which works with children, young people and families in response to social needs.

National Early Years Network (formerly VOLCUF)
77 Holloway Road
London N7 8JZ
☎ 0171 607 9573

The National Early Years Network is the national umbrella organisation for people working with young children and their families. It has a membership of about 1,000 agencies and individuals. The Network provides a wide range of practical activities to develop and enhance services, including a bi-monthly journal, briefing papers and other publications, training workshops and a programme of development and support for local early years forums.

National Playbus Association
AMF House
Whitby Road
Bristol
BS4 3QF
☎ 0117 977 5375

NPA is a national development agency which works directly with all those interested in mobile community provision. It aims to benefit individuals and communities in areas where there is inadequate community provision. Over 250 member projects cover all the major cities and a large number of rural areas.

Pre-school Learning Alliance (PLA)
69 Kings Cross Road
London WC1X 9LL
☎ 0171 833 0991

The PLA is an educational charity and membership organisation promoting quality education and care for pre-school children and support for their families in England. The charity offers national validated training courses, a monthly magazine, *Under Five Contact*, a range of specialist publications, access to grants and an accreditation scheme which ensures high quality provision.

Racial Equality Councils

Most areas have a local community relations council or council for racial equality which will provide local information on organisations and resources. See phone book for address.

Scottish Childminding Association

Room 7
Stirling Business Centre
Wellgreen
Stirling FK8 2DZ
☎ 01786 445377

SCMA exists to promote childminding as a quality childcare service. Its primary purpose is to advise childminders, parents, employers and central and local government on best practice in childminding and how to achieve this.

Scottish Pre-school Play Association

14 Elliot Place
Glasgow G3 8EP
☎ 0141 221 4148

SPPA is an educational charity committed to the development of quality care and education in pre-school groups which respects the rights, responsibilities and needs of all children and their parents.

Wales Pre-school Playgroups Association

2a Chester Street
Wrexham
Clwyd LL13 8BD
☎ 01978 358195

WPPA helps parents understand and provide for the needs of their children; to promote community situations in which parents can, with enjoyment and confidence, use their knowledge and resources in the development of their children and themselves.

Working for Childcare
   77 Holloway Road
   London N7 8JZ
   ☎ 0171 700 0281

Working for Childcare is a membership organisation set up to promote the development of quality childcare which meets the needs of parents in paid work and their children.

Working Group against Racism in Children's Resources (WGARCR)
   460 Wandsworth Road
   London SW8 3LK
   ☎ 0171 627 4594

WGARCR provides:

- guidelines for selecting children's books, toys and childcare/development books.

- a newsletter and resources list (including audio/visual material, organisations, bookshops and suppliers/manufacturers).

- a range of training programmes for providers and practitioners concerned with children's resources.

APPENDIX A

In December 1991 the United Kingdom ratified the United Nations Convention on the Rights of the Child.

The State Parties to the present Convention . . . have agreed as follows:

Article 2

1. States Parties shall respect and ensure the rights set forth in the present Convention to each child within their jurisdiction without discrimination of any kind, irrespective of the child's or his or her parent's or legal guardian's race, colour, sex, language, religion, political or other opinion, national, ethnic or social origin, property, disability, birth or other status.

2. States Parties shall take all appropriate measures to ensure that the child is protected against all forms of discrimination or punishment on the basis of the status, activities, expressed opinions, or beliefs of the child's parents, legal guardians, or family members.

Article 14

1. States Parties shall respect the right of the child to freedom of thought, conscience and religion.

2. States Parties shall respect the rights and duties of the parents and, when applicable, legal guardians, to provide direction to the child in the exercise of his or her right in a manner consistent with the evolving capacities of the child.

3. Freedom to manifest one's religion or beliefs may be subject only to such limitations as are prescribed by law and are

necessary to protect public safety, order, health or morals, or the fundamental rights and freedoms of others.

Article 29

1. States Parties agree that the education of the child shall be directed to:

    (a) The development of the child's personality, talents and mental and physical abilities to their fullest potential;

    (b) The development of respect for human rights and fundamental freedoms, and for the principles enshrined in the Charter of the United Nations;

    (c) The development of respect for the child's parents, his or her own cultural identity, language and values, for the national values of the country in which the child is living, the country from which he or she may originate, and for civilisations different from his or her own;

    (d) The preparation of the child for responsible life in a free society, in the spirit of understanding, peace, tolerance, equality of sexes, and friendship among all peoples, ethnic, national and religious groups and persons of indigenous origin;

    (e) The development of respect for the natural environment.

Article 30

In those States in which ethnic, religious or linguistic minorities or persons of indigenous origin exist, a child belonging to such a minority or who is indigenous shall not be denied the right, in community with other members of his or her group, to enjoy his or her own culture, to profess and practice his or her own religion, or to use his or her own language.

Article 31

1. States Parties recognise the right of the child to rest and leisure, to engage in play and recreational activities approp riate to the age of the child and to participate freely in cultural life and the arts.

2. States Parties shall respect and promote the right of the child to participate fully in cultural and artistic life and shall encourage the provision of appropriate and equal opportun ities for cultural, artistic, recreational and leisure activity.

APPENDIX B

Law Enforcement under the Race Relations Act 1976

The Act provides various forms of legal redress against acts of discrimination: individual complaints, legal action in the CRE's name, and formal investigations conducted by the CRE.

Complaints

Anyone who believes that he or she has suffered discrimination on racial grounds can file a complaint in an industrial tribunal (in employment cases) or initiate proceedings in a county or sheriff court (in education, services, and other non-employment cases).

Complainants may apply to the CRE for assistance in both employment and non-employment cases. Such assistance may include:

- advice

- procuring a settlement

- legal representation.

Help and advice are also available from local racial equality councils – a list is available from the CRE.

Investigations

The CRE has the power under the Race Relations Act to conduct formal investigations into suspected discrimination. If the proposed investigation is into a named institution, the CRE must:

- have grounds for belief that discrimination may have occurred

- issue terms of reference for the investigation

- offer the named institution an opportunity to make representations concerning the proposed investigation.

If an investigation reaches a finding of unlawful discrimination, the CRE may issue a non-discrimination notice, except in cases of public sector education bodies where the Secretary of State has enforcement powers.

Proceedings brought by the CRE

In the case of alleged breaches of Sections 29, 30 and 31 (discriminatory advertisements, and instructions and pressure to discriminate), only the CRE can bring proceedings, which would be heard in a county or sheriff court.

The CRE also has the power to seek judicial review of the decisions or actions of public bodies.

COMMISSION FOR RACIAL EQUALITY

The Commission for Racial Equality was set up by the Race Relations Act 1976 with the duties of:

- Working towards the elimination of discrimination.

- Promoting equality of opportunity and good relations between persons of different racial groups.

- Keeping under review the working of the Act, and, when required by the Secretary of State or when it otherwise thinks it is necessary, drawing up and submitting to the Secretary of State proposals for amending it.

UNITING BRITAIN

COMMISSION FOR RACIAL EQUALITY

FOR A JUST SOCIETY

Head Office
Elliot House
10/12 Allington Street
London SW1E 5EH
☎ 0171-828 7022

Birmingham
Alpha Tower (11th floor)
Suffolk Street Queensway
Birmingham B1 1TT
☎ 0121-632 4544

Leeds
Yorkshire Bank Chambers
(1st floor)
Infirmary Street
Leeds LS1 2JP
☎ 0113-243 4413

Leicester
Haymarket House (4th floor)
Haymarket Shopping Centre
Leicester LE1 3YG
☎ 0116-251 7852

Manchester
Maybrook House (5th floor)
40 Blackfriars Street
Manchester M3 2EG
☎ 0161-831 7782

Scotland
45 Hanover Street
Edinburgh EH2 2PJ
☎ 0131-226 5186

Wales
Pearl Assurance House
(14th floor)
Greyfriars Street
Cardiff CF1 3AG
☎ 01222-388977